Rulers and Rebels

Navigating the Intricate Web of Power, Government, and Social Dynamism

The Curious Philosopher

Copyright Page

Disclaimer

The views and opinions expressed in this book are those of the author(s) and do not necessarily reflect the official policy or position of any other agency, organization, employer, or company. The contents of this book are for informational and educational purposes only and are not intended to serve as professional advice, diagnosis, or treatment.

The information provided in this book is believed to be accurate and reliable as of the date of publication. However, it may include some errors or inaccuracies, and no warranty or guarantee is provided regarding the accuracy, timeliness, or applicability of the content.

Readers are encouraged to consult with professional philosophers, educators, or other qualified professionals where appropriate for personalized advice. The author(s) and publisher shall not be liable for any loss, damage, or harm caused or alleged to be caused, directly or indirectly, by the information or ideas contained, suggested, or referenced in this book.

By reading this book, the reader acknowledges and agrees that they are solely responsible for how they interpret and apply the information contained herein.

This book may also include references to other works, studies, and sources. These references are provided for further reading and exploration and do not imply endorsement or validation of the specific theories, viewpoints, or interpretations presented in those works.

Chapter 1: Introduction

Have you ever wondered why we have governments and what their purpose is? Or how societies decide who gets to make the rules and who has to follow them? If so, then you've ventured into the realm of political philosophy!

A. Definition of Political Philosophy

At its core, political philosophy is the study of questions related to government, power, and social systems. It's a field that has fascinated thinkers for thousands of years, and it encompasses a wide range of topics, from the role of the state to the rights and duties of citizens.

B. Purpose of Political Philosophy

The main goal of political philosophy is to help us better understand the complex web of relationships and dynamics that make up our societies. By studying the works of great political philosophers and analyzing different types of governments and social systems, we can gain valuable insights into how societies function and how we can improve them.

C. Scope of the Book

In this book, we will explore the fascinating world of political philosophy together. We'll start by looking at the roots of political philosophy in ancient civilizations and the writings of Greek philosophers. From there, we'll delve into the study of government, examining different forms of government and the concept of the social contract. We'll also explore the dynamics of power, looking at how power is distributed and how it can be abused. Finally, we'll take a closer look at social systems and their impact on individuals and societies as a whole.

So, whether you're a student of political philosophy, or just someone who's curious about how societies work, this book is for you! Let's dive in and discover the fascinating world of political philosophy together!

Chapter 2: The Roots of Political Philosophy

Ever wonder how our ideas about government and society came to be? To answer that, we need to take a trip back in time and explore the roots of political philosophy!

A. Ancient Civilizations

In ancient civilizations, leaders and thinkers began to ponder the best ways to organize society. In places like Egypt and Mesopotamia, rulers created laws and systems to maintain order. While these early societies didn't have political philosophy in the way we think of it today, their efforts laid the groundwork for future thinkers.

B. The Greek Philosophers

The real boom of political philosophy began with the Greek philosophers. These guys were the rock stars of their time, asking big questions about life, government, and society. One of the most famous was Socrates, who challenged people to question their beliefs and seek wisdom. His student, Plato, wrote about the ideal society, imagining a world governed by philosopher-kings. Another student of Socrates, Aristotle, also had a lot to say about government, arguing for a balanced approach that avoided extremes.

C. Medieval Political Thought

Fast forward a few hundred years, and we land in the medieval era. During this time, religion played a big role in shaping people's ideas about government. The Catholic Church, in particular, had a lot of influence, and thinkers like St. Augustine and St. Thomas Aquinas wrote about the relationship between church and state.

D. Renaissance and Enlightenment

As we move into the Renaissance and Enlightenment, we see a shift towards more secular (non-religious) ideas. Thinkers like Machiavelli and Hobbes wrote about the nature of power and the need for strong rulers. Others, like Locke and Rousseau, emphasized the importance of individual rights and the social contract, which is the idea that people agree to follow certain rules in exchange for protection and order.

So, from ancient civilizations to the Enlightenment, political philosophy has a long and rich history that has shaped the way we think about government and society today. And as we'll see in the next chapters, these ideas continue to influence us in the modern world. So, stay tuned!

Chapter 3: The Study of Government

Welcome to our journey into the fascinating world of government! In this chapter, we will uncover the different ways societies organize themselves, and explore the relationships between individuals, societies, and the state.

A. Forms of Government

Governments come in all shapes and sizes. There are monarchies, where kings and queens rule, and democracies, where the people get a say in how things are run. There are also systems where a few people hold all the power, like in an oligarchy, and others where the government controls everything, like in a communism. Each form has its own way of doing things, but the goal is generally the same - to maintain order and help society run smoothly.

B. The Social Contract

The social contract is a really cool idea that's been around for a while. It's like an invisible agreement between the people and the government. The idea is that people agree to follow the rules and laws of society, and in return, the government protects them and keeps things in order. It's like a trade-off - we give up some freedom to live in a safe and orderly society.

C. The Role of the State

The state, or the government, has a big job. It needs to make and enforce laws, protect the country from outside threats, and provide services like education and healthcare. It's like a big umbrella that covers and protects society, making sure everything runs smoothly and people are treated fairly.

D. Government's Relationship with the Individual

This is where things can get a bit tricky. On one hand, the government needs to have some control to maintain order. But on the other hand, people value their freedom and don't want the government to have too much power. It's a delicate balance, and different governments handle it in different ways. In a democracy, for example, the people have more say in how things are run, which can help keep the government in check.

So, as we can see, the study of government is a rich and complex field that covers everything from the types of government to the social contract and the relationship between the individual and the state. In the next chapter, we will delve deeper into the dynamics of power and explore how power is used and abused in society. Stay tuned!

Chapter 4: The Dynamics of Power

Ever noticed how some people or groups seem to call the shots, while others follow? This chapter is all about understanding power, a force that shapes our societies in big ways.

A. Definition of Power

Simply put, power is the ability to influence or control the actions of others. It's like the energy that fuels the engine of society, driving decisions and actions at every level.

B. Types of Power

Power comes in many forms. There's the power that comes from having a position of authority, like a president or a boss. There's also the power that comes from knowledge and ideas, like a scientist or a writer. And don't forget the power of persuasion, where people use their charisma and communication skills to influence others. Each type of power plays a role in shaping society.

C. The Distribution of Power

In any society, power is distributed among different groups and individuals. Some people have a lot of power, while others have very little. This distribution can be based on things like wealth, social status, or age. The way power is distributed can tell us a lot about a society's values and priorities.

D. The Abuse of Power

Unfortunately, power isn't always used for the greater good. Sometimes, people abuse their power to take advantage of others or to maintain their own position. This can lead to injustice and inequality, and it's something that societies have to guard against.

In conclusion, power is a fascinating and complex force that shapes our societies in many ways. By understanding the dynamics of power, we can better navigate our own lives and work towards creating a more just and equitable society. In the next chapter, we'll take a closer look at social systems and their impact on individuals and societies as a whole. Stay tuned!

Chapter 5: Social Systems and Their Impact

Ever wondered why we organize ourselves in the way we do? Well, you're in the right place! In this chapter, we're going to explore social systems and their big impact on our lives.

A. Definition of Social Systems

At its core, a social system is just a fancy term for the organized way that society is structured. Think of it as the rules and roles that help keep everything running smoothly. This includes things like family, education, religion, and more.

B. Types of Social Systems

There are many different types of social systems out there, each playing a unique role in society. For example, the family is a social system that helps raise and care for children. Education is another social system that helps teach new generations valuable skills and knowledge. And let's not forget about religion, which provides spiritual guidance and brings communities together.

C. The Interaction between Social Systems and Government

Social systems and government are like two peas in a pod. They work together to create a stable and functioning society. The government creates laws and rules that help support social systems, like funding for education or protections for families. In turn, social systems help shape the values and norms that influence government policies.

D. The Impact of Social Systems on Individuals

Social systems have a big impact on us as individuals. They shape our values, beliefs, and behaviors. They also provide us with support and a sense of belonging. But sometimes, social systems can also be limiting, especially if they're rigid or discriminatory. It's important for us to be aware of how social systems shape our lives and to work towards creating more inclusive and equitable systems for everyone.

So, as we've seen, social systems are a vital part of society that shape our lives in many ways. By understanding how these systems work, we can better navigate our own lives and work towards creating a more just and harmonious society. Stay tuned for our next chapter, where we'll explore contemporary political philosophy and its impact on our world today.

Chapter 6: Contemporary Political Philosophy

In our ever-changing world, political philosophy continues to evolve and adapt. Let's dive into the modern era and see how political thought has shaped the 20th and 21st centuries.

A. 20th and 21st Century Thought

The last century has seen a tremendous shift in political philosophy, with new ideas and theories emerging. Thinkers like John Rawls focused on justice and fairness, developing ideas on how societies can be more equitable. Other philosophers, like Hannah Arendt, examined the nature of power and how it can be used or abused. These thoughts have shaped our understanding of democracy, human rights, and much more.

B. Major Political Movements

Political movements have always been a driving force for change. In the 20th century, we saw the rise of civil rights movements, feminist movements, and much more. These movements have fought for equality, justice, and freedom, challenging old ways of thinking and pushing society to evolve. They've paved the way for many of the rights and freedoms we enjoy today.

C. The Future of Political Philosophy

As we look to the future, political philosophy will continue to play a vital role in shaping our world. New challenges, such as climate change, global inequality, and the rise of new technologies, will require us to think critically about how we organize our societies. Political philosophy will help us navigate these complex issues and work towards a more just and sustainable world.

In conclusion, contemporary political philosophy is a vibrant and dynamic field that has a profound impact on our world. By exploring new ideas and learning from past movements, we can continue to evolve and build a better future for everyone. Stay tuned for our next chapter, where we'll delve into case studies that bring these concepts to life.

Chapter 7: Hypothetical Case Studies

Now that we've explored the ins and outs of political philosophy, let's put our knowledge to the test with some hypothetical case studies. Don't worry, we'll keep it simple and engaging!

A. Historical Examples

Imagine we're traveling back in time to ancient Greece, where democracy was born. Picture a society where citizens gathered to make decisions collectively. But wait, there's a catch! Not everyone was considered a citizen. Women, slaves, and non-landowners were excluded from the decision-making process. What does this tell us about the limitations of early democratic systems?

B. Modern Day Examples

Now, let's jump back into the present. Consider a modern democratic country where everyone has the right to vote. It sounds perfect, right? But hold on, there are still challenges. What about the influence of money in politics, or the role of the media in shaping public opinion?

These are all important factors that can affect how power is distributed and exercised in a democracy.

C. Comparative Analysis

Finally, let's compare our two examples. On the surface, ancient Greece and a modern democracy might seem worlds apart. But when we dig deeper, we see that there are some common themes. In both cases, the question of who has a voice and who doesn't is central to the discussion. And in both cases, we see that external factors, like wealth or media, can influence the democratic process.

By looking at these hypothetical case studies, we can see how the principles of political philosophy play out in real-world scenarios. They help us understand the complexities of government, power, and society, and they give us valuable insights that we can use to navigate our own lives and work towards a better future. So, keep these examples in mind as you continue to explore the fascinating world of political philosophy!

Chapter 8: Conclusion

As we wrap up our journey through the world of political philosophy, let's take a moment to reflect on the key concepts we've explored and the importance of this fascinating field.

A. Summary of Key Concepts

We've traveled through time, from ancient civilizations to the modern day, to understand how political philosophy has evolved. We've delved into the workings of government, the dynamics of power, and the impact of social systems on individuals and society as a whole. Along the way, we've encountered great thinkers like Plato, Aristotle, and John Rawls, and we've tackled big ideas like democracy, the social contract, and human rights.

B. The Importance of Political Philosophy

So, why does all this matter? Political philosophy is not just an academic exercise; it's a vital tool that helps us navigate the complexities of our world. It helps us understand the structures that shape our lives and the values that guide our societies. It empowers us to be informed citizens, capable of making thoughtful decisions and contributing to the collective good. In short, political philosophy is essential because it helps us make sense of the world and our place in it.

In conclusion, our exploration of political philosophy has given us a solid foundation for understanding the key concepts and ideas that shape our world. But remember, this is just the beginning! The field of political philosophy is vast and ever-evolving, and there's always more to learn. So, keep questioning, keep exploring, and keep striving for a deeper understanding of the world around you. The journey may be challenging, but the rewards are well worth it.

About The Curious Philosopher

Welcome to The Curious Philosopher, your dedicated platform for diving deep into the world of philosophy. We are more than just a YouTube channel or a book publisher. We are a beacon of enlightenment, making complex philosophical concepts accessible and engaging for all.

Our YouTube channel is a rich repository of philosophy made simple. We take the profound and often complex ideas from the world of philosophy and break them down into digestible, easy-to-understand content. From the ancient wisdom of Socrates to the existentialist thoughts of Sartre, we cover a broad spectrum of philosophical schools and thoughts, making philosophy accessible to everyone, regardless of their background or prior knowledge.

As a book publisher, we take the same approach, transforming intricate philosophical theories into comprehensible narratives. Our books are not just collections of words, but vessels of wisdom that make philosophy approachable and relatable. We believe that philosophy should not be confined to academic circles, but should be available to all who seek to understand the world and their place in it.

At The Curious Philosopher, we believe in the power of curiosity and the pursuit of knowledge. We are here to stoke the fires of your curiosity, to guide you on your intellectual journey, and to help you navigate the fascinating world of philosophy.

If you are someone who is not afraid to question, to explore, and to learn, then you are in the right place. Join us on this journey of exploration, as we make philosophy easy to understand, one concept at a time.

Be sure to visit our Youtube channel at:

https://www.curiousphilosopher.com/youtube

You can also visit us on the web at

https://www.curiousphilosopher.com

Welcome to The Curious Philosopher. Stay curious. Stay enlightened.

9 798865 943525